Risking Hope

Fragile Faith in the Healing Process

Expanded Edition

Kathleen O'Connell Chesto

Sheed & Ward

Sheed & Ward™ is a service of the National Catholic
Reporter Publishing Company, Inc.

Library of Congress Catalog Card Number: 89-64498

ISBN: 1-55612-322-1

Published by: Sheed & Ward
                115 E. Armour Blvd. P.O. Box 419492
                Kansas City, MO 64141

To order, call: (800) 333-7373

Second printing, 1996.

Contents

Introduction

This is a story about healing. Oh, not the spectacular kind of healing for which we usually reserve the title miracle, (if one more person asks me if I have been to Father DiOrio, read Bernie Seigel, or "really asked God to heal me," I will hit her or him with my cane) but it is healing, nonetheless. Not all miracles are physical and some of the most dramatic healings slip by us unnoticed in our search for the extraordinary.

In January of 1986, my sister and her husband were in a motorcycle accident near their home in Guatemala. He lost a leg and the use of one of his arms; her leg was shattered. While their lives hung in delicate balance, my Mom and I flew down to be with them, turning in desperation to the United States Embassy to help us find blood donors, decent hospitals and good medical care.

Reluctantly, I returned to my family and my job, leaving my mother to offer support and to keep the rest of us informed with almost daily phone calls. It is important to this story to understand the sense of dread and spiritual anguish that was suffocating our family in the wake of this tragedy. There is never a good time to learn that you have a degenerative illness, but some times are definitely worse than others.

The trip had left me physically exhausted, emotionally drained and spiritually angry, a good candidate for the flu running rampant in our community. I spent most of February in bed with a raging fever, the joyful news that Dina and Mac would survive barely penetrating the haze. I was not well enough to begin to comprehend the terrible price survival sometimes demands. On March 1, I awoke to discover my legs had grown terribly heavy and completely numb.

The first hospitalization followed, but the tests were all negative. I returned home and even went back to my job, though I soon needed a wheelchair to get around the large diocesan center. The doctor's nonchalance in the face of this increasing paralysis was terrifying. My family simply tried to ignore what was happening; they had had all they could bear. By mid-April the numbness had spread upward to my chest. When my bladder and bowel control failed and my breathing became compromised, I was admitted to the neuro-intensive care unit at Yale-New Haven Hospital.

This is where the story begins. The following pages are a journal I kept from that first night in intensive care up to the present. It is the record of my own struggle with the unwelcome verdict of progressive multiple sclerosis and the devastating impact it had on my family. It is a story of denial, depression, fear, guilt and suicide, but more importantly, it is a story of healing and hope.

Looking back over this period of my life, it seemed to fall into four general phases. I have begun to think of the time from March to August of 1986 as The Crisis, the time when I was diagnosed and hospitalized four times, returning home each time with a little less mobility. My children, Jon, Becky and Liz were fifteen, thirteen and nine, respectively. Each hospitalization left them a little more traumatized, despite the heroic efforts of my husband Ed to keep their lives functioning normally. Crisis was followed by a period of Denial. I returned to my doctoral studies, my job as assistant diocesan director of religious education, and tried to pick up my life as if nothing had happened. My body eventually succumbed to the debilitating fatigue so common with MS and I was forced to recognize that I could no longer live as I had always lived. Depression came with that realization and with resignation from my job. Only after sufficient grieving was I able to begin Letting Go of what could no longer be, and concentrating on what is.

I have divided the journal according to these stages, but it did not happen as neatly as I have described. Life is seldom neat and rarely can it be relied upon to catalog cleanly. The stages, as I experienced them, tended to overlap each other. I did not complete one phase, bringing it into some kind of resolution, before moving into the next, but carried much of the pain of the earlier into the later. Each new crisis, each new discovery of advancing paralysis, is capable of again precipitating the same cycle.

This little book is not intended as a clear-cut outline of the stages of adjustment to disability and degenerative disease. It is much more a Monday morning quarterback's attempt to make sense out of Sunday's game. Nor is it a "How-To" manual on coping with pain and loss; it contains no answers. It is, rather, my own personal journey with suffering and the questions I encounter in the ongoing struggle for survival.

I share these thoughts with you in the hope that you, the reader, will recognize on these pages your own pain, and be comforted.

Crisis

"All great truths begin as blasphemies."
—George Bernard Shaw

. . . to Ed

Twilight

It is twilight. The dim, half-light traces oblique shadows on white walls. The eerie silence is broken only by the faint humming, wheezing, and occasional beeping of machinery. I have discovered there is no night in intensive care, only this strange, simulated dusk, stretching endlessly toward dawn.

A white blanket is spread neatly over me. Only my eyes reveal its presence. There is no sensation to tell me if it is heavy, or warm. Ominously, a respirator clutches the bedrailings. The IV counter makes a gentle ticking sound as it monitors the passage of the burning liquid into my veins. Strange, a terrible fire rages inside my body, yet, outside, it is numb.

An acrid taste lingers in my mouth. What on earth did I eat? Slowly, I review the evening: the emergency room, the spinal tap and the searing pain, Ed's tears falling on my face as he held me down, the mylegram, more spinal taps, more pain and still more tests. I ate nothing. The taste is fear.

Unwelcome images do battle against sleep. They come—the toddler, the little girl struggling with her sister's two-wheeler, the nine-year-old conquering the oak tree in the back yard, the teenager flying across the ice, the nun, the teacher, the young mother, all strangely active, yet, all in mocking slow motion. It isn't their fluidity of movement that taunts me, it is the bond between their motion and their essence. Who will I be when I can no longer move? Who will I be when the things that have defined me to myself are no longer possible?

It is not losing my legs or arms that fills me with fear so tangible that I can taste it. Tonight, in the ICU twilight, I am afraid of losing myself.

4/20/86

Passover

It is the feast of Passover. The neurology floor is almost emptied of doctors. It feels incongruous, an unfitting celebration for those whose lives reflect unlimited faith in science, but then, how many of us ever live what we celebrate?

There is much to be said
For sprinkling blood
On doorposts
For asking the questions,
Revering the myths
That protect the home
As the angel of death
Passes over.

Never forget, O Physician!
It is not enough
That you should know
The many masks the angel wears—
Not enough
That you should know
The tools of deathly combat—
To win.

For victory lies also
In knowing well
The lifeblood that guards the lintel
And bids the angel of death
"Pass over!"

4/21/86

Threatened

I was molested as a child. The body I had thought was mine was powerless in the hands of the intruder. More terrifying than anything that was done to me was the fear of what might yet happen. I was left, alone, and physically unharmed, but a nameless face haunted my childhood dreams.

Once again the molester comes, no longer a nameless face, but a faceless name. Once again my body is threatened—my body!—and I am outraged and powerless. There is no way of knowing what capricious whim will attack me next. Once again, I am a child, crying, terrified, in the dark.

4/23/86

Alone

Today, I am alone. I would not have thought one could feel so alone with a roommate in the next bed, countless nurses and aids on the floor, and doctors wandering to and fro. The noise from the corridor invades the room, but I am alone.

Yesterday was the final, conclusive test, the one that would provide us with the ANSWER: degenerative disease or simple virus. I carried the results back to the neurology floor myself in an ominous brown envelope. Three doctors met me, snatched the all-revealing films from my hands, and rushed to the consultation room. They never came back, and today, I am alone.

I thought that they would tell me this morning. Every morning, the chief of neurology, two residents, and a hoard of students visit me, stick pins in my body to see how far the paralysis has advanced, and discuss my "case" as if I were a cadaver on a slab in the morgue. Today, no one came.

The nurses asked all morning if the doctors had come yet. With each successive negative response, they averted their eyes more quickly and vanished more rapidly, terrified of the question I might ask. Soon, they stopped coming. This afternoon, I am alone while walls of silence grow rapidly around me. If it were not for the anguish on the faces of those forced to walk by me, I would swear I have become invisible.

Please, don't do this to me! I need a hand to hold, a shoulder to cry on. I promise I won't ask the question. There is no need to ask the question. Your silence screams the answer your lips are afraid to speak.

4/25/86

Why . . .

"Never forget, you are filling up what is wanting in the sufferings of Christ."

I raised my eyes from the bed to the episcopal cross at his waist, the heavy gold chain stretched across his chest, the gray beard, the gentle, dark eyes, filled with compassion. I wonder—would it be a sacrilege to throw a bed pan at a bishop?

Are your words supposed to comfort me? It isn't enough, that God would condemn his own son to a brutal death, but God wants me to be miserable also? Why has your God, whom you tell me can forgive all, set the price of sin so high?

Is my illness so frightening, my paralysis so terrifying to you that you would accept an answer at any cost? I reject your answer and your God, as I reject my own question. There can be no "Why"; there is no reason. Better to live forever with the mystery in the presence of an inscrutable God, than rest secure for one moment in the hands of a vengeful One.

5/2/86

Mystery

The problem with the Christian Church is that we named all the wrong things mystery. I have no trouble believing in the Trinity. I am at least six different people in the course of any given day. That God should choose to be three does not even surprise me, let alone cause a crisis in my faith.

I don't have any trouble believing in Incarnation, either. Even if I had never known Jesus, I have seen enough divinity in all the humanity around me, that Incarnation causes me no problems.

But the idea that an all-good, all-loving, all-powerful God, if there is such a God, could allow good people to suffer, now that's a mystery. Strange, isn't it, that this is the mystery we should work so hard to explain?

5/3/86

INA

My roommate left today. Hers was not the common, joyful departure I have witnessed so frequently in the last month. Her frail little body, usually carried with such pride, was bent and old. Her sparkling blue eyes, reddened by a night of weeping, had turned dull and lifeless. What is the difference between hope and despair? You come to a hospital to get well. You go to a nursing home to die.

5/7/86

Crocus Stumps

I missed the crocuses. I found the stumps of stalks today, decapitated by the lawnmower, but they had long been dead. I was in intensive care when they first pushed through the still-frozen ground. I had started the intra-venous ACTH when the first leaves appeared. I was walking the bars in physical therapy by the time the blossoms withered. Why couldn't they have waited for me?

It had been a golden autumn day when I planted them. My job was new, my career finally getting off the ground. It seemed there would be a hundred springs to enjoy my flowers.

They say I have adjusted well to the canes, the mobility device, the occasional catheters. They say I have accepted the disease and its limitations beautifully. If I have adjusted so well and accepted so much, then tell me, why am I sitting on the ground among the crocus stumps, crying?

5/18/86

Reciprocal God

I think I have lost my God. I used to believe in a reciprocal God: I did the right things and said the right prayers and God did what I asked. It isn't working any more; God doesn't play fair. The Great Score-Keeper in the Sky has lost count. I must be at least five down.

I can no longer pray to be healed. I cannot pray to change God, or even to change what is. But perhaps I can still pray to change me. Perhaps there is a God somewhere beyond my manipulation who will answer.

"I am the Lord, your God, you shall not have strange gods before me."

5/21/86

It Helps!

Today was one of those days. My legs were bad: the canes were not enough support and I crashed on the couch, unwillingly giving in to the need to rest. My guitar was no comfort. Do you know how a guitar sounds when your left hand isn't working? It goes "Flub, flub." My twitching nerves refused to let my eyes focus on the music and I finally flung the book across the room in frustration.

Once started, I couldn't seem to stop. Book after book followed the first one across the living room as I shouted: "I hate it! I hate living like this! I would rather be dead!"

My eyes met Ed's as he sat quietly on the hearth, and I turned away in shame. Now I would get the lecture anyone could see I deserved. I should be grateful; after all, I *was* alive. I could walk again with canes; my bladder was functioning, I could see, I could breathe on my own. Anyone would have reminded me of how fortunate I had been.

But this wasn't anyone; it was Ed. He walked slowly across the room, picking up one of the music books as he came.

"Want to throw it again?" he asked, putting it gently in my lap.

I couldn't help grinning through my tears. His arms closed tightly around me, his tears mingling with my own as he said gently: "If it helps at all, I love you."

It helps. Oh God, how it helps!

5/30/86

Nite Lite

Elizabeth came to my room during the night, body rigid with a fear beyond tears, nine-year-old eyes grown suddenly old.

"Mommy, I'm afraid. I'm so afraid my tummy hurts. I dreamed that when I woke up in the morning you were completely paralyzed."

Child of mine, what cursed intuition brought you to my side tonight? Did you sense my fear as my hands trembled with the dishes at the supper table? Did you hear my frustration as my fingers stumbled across the piano keys? Do my eyes reveal the pain I never speak? How did the anguish I have worked so hard to keep from you invade your dreams?

"Elizabeth, do you remember when you were little and you were afraid of the dark? I couldn't take away your fear. That is the terrible thing about fear. It lives deep inside of us and we are the only ones who can conquer it. But I could take away the dark.

"Let me be your nite lite now. We can talk, and we can cry, and we can hold each other tight, until the dark is a little brighter and both of us can cope."

6/1/86

Woman?

Ellie took me to have my colors done. I am a "summer" and so is she. We experimented with the make-up, laughing like teenagers, parading before the mirror. She even bought me a shirt in "our colors."

Is it possible to feel like a woman again, despite the canes and the chair? Trust Ellie to find a way to ignite a little spark of feminine vanity and make me feel better.

6/7/86

Please Help Me

My other friends have all deserted me. No one calls or visits or even drops a card. Their lives have moved on while mine has come to a grinding halt. I think I make them uncomfortable, a constant reminder of their own mortality and human fragility. Please, please, don't be scared away. I need you. Is that what makes it so scary? Have I always been the giver, the leaned-on one? I know my illness is difficult for you, but it's not a picnic for me either. I can't do it alone. Help me, please help me.

6/10/86

In the Way

Once again, Becky got the brunt of my anger. I lashed out at her for—God knows what! I think I even called her names. She came back to me later, tears streaming down her cheeks.

"Mommy, it hurts me when you do that. Why are you so angry with me?"

My arms reached out to her as I begged God to help her find it in her fourteen-year-old heart to forgive me.

"I'm not angry with you, Love. I am angry with the disease, I am angry with the paralysis, I am angry with life. You just got in the way."

6/25/86

Betrayed

Blood clots! O treacherous legs! For 41 years you have served me so well. Why do you continue to betray me, now when I no longer even walk upon you?

7/4/86

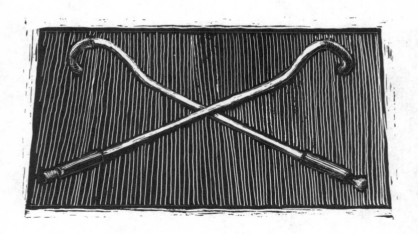

"I don't walk."

A new vascular surgeon visited me today. He explained, in great detail, how no one my age should ever have thrombosis. It was all due to a lack of exercise. I should walk at least two miles a day.

"But Doctor, I don't walk."

"I know you don't," he interjected without making sure he understood my meaning, "that is why you are here." Another lecture on the great value of exercise followed.

"Doctor, I *can't* walk."

"Nonsense!" he interrupted again. "Anyone can walk!"

"Not when you are paralyzed!"

* * *

Doctors could save themselves a great deal of pain and embarassment if they read a patient's chart before entering the room.

7/5/86

Tunneling Out

A large plastic shovel hangs above my hospital bed. I have warned everyone to beware of the trap door at my side. I'm tired of the hospital; I'm tunneling out.

The staff doctor this morning greeted my words with a totally blank expression. "How can you? You're on the ninth floor."

"I'm already down to the fourth, so you'd better watch out!"

Not even a smile.

7/12/86

Why Pray?

I came home yesterday with two canes. I was told to "adjust." The blood clots triggered another exacerbation of the disease, and I am far more disabled than I was when I went into the hospital.

Last night, my nine-year-old approached me with a heart-wrenching question.

"Is God punishing us?" she asked tearfully.

I held her close to me and asked if she thought I would ever cripple her as a punishment. Her response was an instant negative; I loved her too much for that, she was sure. But God loved her, too, I pointed out.

"Well then, why didn't God stop it? You're a good person, Mommy. All you do is go around and teach people about God. Why does God want you crippled?"

I reassured her that God didn't want me crippled, but that didn't answer the Why. The boys who had stolen the car that had crashed into her aunt and uncle had had free will and God wouldn't take that away. Perhaps there was a free will in the illness that had invaded my body. I searched for an answer that would make sense. She considered it for a long time before she said solemnly:

"If God didn't cause it, and God can't stop it, why pray?"

My question precisely, Little One! Are you old enough to understand I no longer pray to change God, I pray to change me?

7/21/86

Denial

The biggest problem with dishonesty is that we may begin to believe our own lies.

. . . to Jon, Becky and Liz

Remission

Such a tentative word! It contains none of the joy of "recovery," none of the hope of "cure." Remission. An oasis in the desert, a moment of rest before the perilous journey continues.

9/1/86

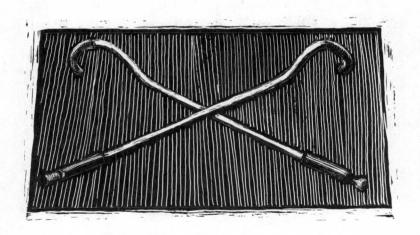

"Arise and Walk!"

I did my first workshop today since becoming sick. The Protestant ministers all knew me, but they did not know me with canes. The trip across the stage seemed to take forever, my dragging feet and thumping canes echoing loudly on the hollow wooden surface. Everyone breathed a sigh of relief as I balanced my canes and myself against the podium and began.

"Wham!" The first cane fell with a resounding crash. One hundred anxious people leaned forward, uncertain whether to jump up and help me or wait out the moment. Before anyone could do anything, the second cane fell, echoing loudly. A woman in the front row became so flustered that she dropped *her* cane, adding yet another crash.

In the tense moment of silence that followed, I lowered my voice and said in a sonorous whisper: "And a voice came from the heavens, saying: 'Arise and walk!' "

It really is time to stop taking myself so seriously.

9/15/86

Just Crippled

The saleswoman's voice droned on in that tone I have heard far too often since being confined to a wheelchair. It was a mixture of patronizing pity and something else I struggled to identify as her words dripped over me.

Beside me, nine-year-old Liz was growing increasingly more fidgety. She suddenly planted her small body firmly between the saleswoman and me. Hands on her hips, a mounting fury in her voice, she said loudly:

"My Mom's not stupid! She's just crippled!"

That was it! People were treating me as if halving my height had halved my intelligence! Back in the car I asked my daughter,

"Why do you suppose people do that?"

"It's because they're afraid, Mommy. They have to prove to themselves that you are different, that way it can't happen to them."

10/16/86

29

Nine-Year-Old Wisdom

"Just crippled." O God, help me to remember the wisdom in my daughter's words. I am just crippled. Not stupid, not less worthwhile, not less of a person, not some kind of freak, not even sick, "just crippled."

10/17/86

Night

It is night. The comforting sound of Ed's deep, even breathing fills the darkened room. The rest of the household sleeps in silence. Nighttime belongs to the disabled. Sleep makes us all equal, rendering helpless the most able-bodied.

I love the night. Here, in its peaceful blackness I can escape the pressures of the day. There is no one to push for one more exercise in therapy, one more hour of work, one more volunteer assist for the school, one more carpool, one more homework assignment. Here, there is no need to force the smile that protects those around me from my pain, while my body screams out its fatigue. The only presence is Ed's silent warmth. I am free to lie quietly watching the stars come out, while the naked limbs of the hickory tree mark the passage of the moon across the sky.

1/5/87

Thorns and Iron

Becky came home from school and plopped on the end of my bed. Her English assignment for the week was to write about the most memorable day of her life, the one that had exercised the most lasting influence. It was to be described as a day of thorns and iron or a day of gold and roses.

I knew she would write about the day in eighth grade when she had been a winner in a national history day competition. I was silently reflecting on the positive impact it had made on her self-confidence and only half listening to her chatter about the assignment when her words cut through my reverie.

"I'm going to write about the day Dad told us you had multiple sclerosis."

I was overwhelmed by anger and pain. We had struggled to give this child so many beautiful experiences. We had worked at creating happy memories, educational opportunities, faith-filled moments. Why should her most memorable day deal with the pain that had come unbidden into our lives, and from which we had tried so hard to shield her?

As she struggled to put her thoughts into words, I knew beyond any shadow of a doubt that all our efforts to protect her from the impact of my illness had failed.

". . . My Mom had been in the hospital for two weeks and had been sick for much longer. We presumed, as all kids do, that nothing could be seriously wrong. Bad things only happen to other people. They weren't supposed to happen to me. I wasn't at all prepared for the day my Dad told us that my Mom had multiple sclerosis.

"When my Mom came home barely walking, I had to assume responsibility for many of the things she used to do for me. Not only did I have to be more independent, but I also had to be more dependable for my Mom and my family. At first, I hated doing laundry and fixing meals and being home for my little sister. But as I began to realize how important I was to my family, it made me feel good about myself. Going places with my Mom has made me sensitive to how difficult it is for handicapped people in our society to be able to do the things the rest of us take for granted. I have learned to be more considerate, not just of my Mom, but of anybody who is having a hard time.

"In some ways, though, I am not as sensitive. I am not as quick to believe everything is my fault. When my Mom came home from the hospital, she seemed to be angry at me most of the time, and I thought it was my fault. After a while, through long talks with her, I began to understand that she was angry at the sickness, not at me. Now when someone acts angry, I try to figure out what's wrong and be helpful instead of assuming it's my fault and getting angry back.

"My Mom is doing better now and can walk without her canes. I don't know why God lets these things happen, but maybe it's because good things can come out of it. We have grown closer as a family. I've become more grown-up and more accepting of life. I know that in the future, I have the strength to handle anything that might happen.

"Even though that day began as a time forged in iron and thorns, it has also brought gold and roses. I guess that's what life is like, a mixture, gold and iron, thorns and roses."

2/9/87

A Deeper Memory

We had an ice-skating party for our family group at the little lake behind the Lyons' home. There is a huge hill sloping down to the pond and everyone brought sleds as well as skates. The fire on the edge of the ice kept the hot chocolate and coffee warm for the skaters and attracted the less daring adults.

Ed knelt by the side of the lake and carefully tied my skates. Neither of us mentioned the fact that there was an excellent chance I would not be able to stand up on them. I looked down on the salt and pepper curls remembering the winter of the skating rink and the countless times he had tied skates on my feet.

It was the winter after Becky was born and I was enmeshed in a critical post-partum depression. Ed had rejected hospitalizing me and had arranged to have people with me during the day. He would return from work each afternoon, bundle me up, and drag me out to the rink he had constructed in the back yard. Sitting me on the back steps, he would tie my skates, just as he was doing now, and push me out on the ice. There, my love of skating took over and I came alive again. It took weeks of patient caring, but slowly, the life seeped back into the rest of my day.

As Ed stood, I hugged him gratefully. His dark eyes told me that he, too, had been remembering, and he grinned. How, I wonder, can you continue to love someone who has brought such pain into your life?

We struggled out to the ice together. MS has done a real number on my sense of balance, and at first, walking in the skates seemed impossible. Once I was moving, though, an older instinct, a deeper memory, seemed to take over. I had forced myself to forget how much I love to skate. Now, with the wind in my face and the sound of my blades scraping the smooth surface, I remembered. I was skating! As long as I kept going in a counter-clockwise circle, I could move. As soon as I turned clock-wise, I fell. I decided it would be wiser not to attempt any spins or jumps. It was enough just to be flying across the ice again.

I will treasure the memory of this day: the smell of the fire and the hot dogs cooking over it; the gray skies, white ice, and naked trees crowding around the pond; the laughter of the adults and children delighting in each other's company; but most of all, the wonderful feeling of motion. I will tuck it away, insurance against a day when there may be only memories.

2/19/87

Tired

I am tired of being good.

I am tired of pretending it doesn't matter.

I am tired of being well-adjusted.

I am tired of the canes.

I am tired of feeling the burden of making others comfortable with my handicap.

I am tired of feeling guilty for the burdens I have placed on my family.

I am tired of trying to accomplish as much as those around me whose bodies function so much better than mine.

I am tired of receiving dirty looks for parking in the handicapped spot on days my handicap is less visible.

I am tired of smiling.

I am tired of not complaining.

I am tired of being terrified of the future.

I am tired of protecting my family from my pain.

I am tired of being tired.

O God, I am so damn tired.

3/6/87

Out of Time

We thought we had time. We saved for a future, for an active retirement that, now, will never be ours. It does not really matter. The astronomical medical bills have decimated the savings.

I wish I had gone to Ireland when I'd had the chance. I wish I had gone to meet all my father's family who remained behind; I wish I had sought out my roots while I was still able to do it. I wish I had gone to Dublin to meet the people using my program and to do the training session for them.

I don't remember voicing the thoughts, but I must have, because here we are at the bank, refinancing the mortgage. Ed is persuasive. By the time we would save the money for such a trip, I will probably not be well enough to go. Ed is a realist. He refuses to cry over the past or hope blindly in the future. Life is happening today. The only time we have is now.

Not only are we going to Ireland, we are going to England and Wales and we are taking the kids!

3/30/87

Forgetting

I am losing my memory. I open my mouth to speak but I can no longer find the word to express the thought. It is there, stored somewhere in the computer banks of my mind, but the pathname has been erased. I can no longer retrieve it.

Events fall into a jumble as my mind refuses to sort and file properly. I call someone, only to forget the reason for my call, or perhaps, even the person's name. Most terrifying of all, though, are the sudden blanks in my short term memory. I "awake" in places, having no idea how I got there, why I am there, or where I am going, the events of the previous hours having been effectively erased.

I could live without my legs, my arms, my eyes, but not without my mind! I hate this disease! You have taken away any possibility of a future, distorted and disfigured my present. Must you now also rob me of my past?

4/10/87

Almost Human

Ed lowered the seat on my bike and I am learning to ride again. I take it to the end of the driveway, sit on the seat and let my feet drag on the ground. There is just a slight incline on the fifty foot stretch of pavement, so a small push will set me rolling. Today I was able to put both feet on the pedals and actually balance. I felt the way I did when I first took off alone across the ice. Almost human.

4/28/87

Advice

Consider, for a moment, the billions of dollars that have been spent on researching the causes and cure for MS. Some of the greatest minds in the world are in the field of auto-immune disease, particularly since the AIDS scare has brought the immune system into the limelight. If none of these people, with all of their elaborate funding and learning, has been able to figure out what to do for MS, why are there so many people within my immediate acquaintance who are absolutely certain that they know the cause, the cure, or both?

I have been badgered with books and tapes, diets and therapies, and a score of armchair psychiatrists who feel perfectly free to analyze every word that comes out of my mouth. Most of us are reasonably careful about interfering in the lives of those who are well. We feel, and rightly so, that what they eat, how they exercise, what they do for entertainment, and how they raise their kids, is none of our business. But there is something about illness, or depression, or both, that makes us terribly vulnerable. Family and friends feel it is not only their right, but their duty, to tell us how to live.

The pseudo-psychiatrists are the worst. "Have you noticed just how much your emotions affect your mobility? You can't let things get to you!" (I should just "get happy," right? It is perfectly all right for you to be depressed, but because I have a degenerative illness, I am required to be happy

100% of the time.) This group is ready to point out all that is lacking in my relationships with my husband, my children, my friends, as well as what might be lacking in my own self-image. The fact that I have become ill is seen as some type of psychological failure, from which their advice will help deliver me. While their observations are frequently correct, they are always destructive.

The physical therapists are certain that whatever exercise has made them strong or fast, or helped them to recover from heart problems, ulcers, or God knows what, will also make me strong again. It does not help to explain that I can't get overheated. What does help is letting them know that I do therapy. I do not tell them about the exercises, though. I suspect they would laugh if they saw me lifting my leg, pillow case draped over the ankle, tuna can in each side!

The dieters are the most intrusive. People I hardly know have called me on the phone to recommend, no, to insist on diets. I must admit to not trying any of them. If I could have a cook, perhaps it would work, but most of these diets involve more thought and preparation than I am willing to put into eating. People are so convinced that if I just eliminated dairy products, or gave up carbohydrates, stopped wheat, or avoided red meat, I would be well. They suspect, when I refuse, that I really don't want to be well. What I don't want is to spend the greater portion of every day thinking about being sick, as I prepare my esoteric meals.

There are times when I feel like a wounded animal above whom the vultures have already begun to gather. I cannot listen any more. I know these people love me, but for now, I cannot bear their love. If I had heeded half their words, I would long since be dead from exhaustion, starvation or suicide. On my tombstone would be the telling epitaph:

Of Kathy, let these words suffice:
Lived with MS, died from advice.

5/7/87

Divorce

We sit at a table, Ed and I, calmly discussing divorce. This man, with whom I promised "forever!" We have survived traumatic births, miscarriages, postpartum depressions, creating a business, building a home, raising children, anger, jealousies, and deep hurt without ever considering anything less than "forever." But today, we discuss divorce; we talk about what could prove to be our only economic solution, should I ever require a long term care facility. I would get medicare; the house would not be taken to meet the bills. What kind of medical system is it that destroys our reasons for living in order to financially sustain the life support systems that keep us alive?

I refuse to believe that it could happen. Everything within me screams at the possible destruction of the most important part of my life. Why am I outwardly so calm? We are so sensible. It would not mean the destruction of our love, the end of us, only the legal paper that defines us.

Why is life doing this to us? If there is a God, and I have begun to seriously doubt that this is so, I don't like that God very much.

6/11/87

Notebooks

I have filled one journal and started another. Why am I writing? I suspect I write the things I cannot say, the things I want my friends and family to know, but cannot tell them. Yet, as I read the entries through, I know it is more than that. I write the things I have not yet allowed myself to believe.

Will I ever face the thoughts and speak the words and be free of the need to hide them in the notebooks of my life?

7/1/87

Lost Child

Eastern Airlines misplaced Becky. She was on her way back from Guatamala and we were at the airport to meet her, but she never got off the plane. After some hysterical fighting with the people in the terminal, we finally extracted the information that her flight from Miami had been cancelled. No one could tell us, however, if Becky had ever gotten that far. My sister in Guatamala was unable to reassure us; she had left Becky at the airport, waiting for the plane. The hotel in Miami, where the Eastern travellers were being housed, informed us that Becky had not checked in, but she was not expected, since she was underage.

We called my parents, just in case Becky had tried to reach someone. My Mom quickly contacted Dora Trujullo, the U.S. Consulate General, and a Marine Search of the Guatemala airport was initiated. Eastern continued to be unhelpful. There had been a late evening flight from Miami to Boston, but a passenger list would be available only if the plane went down!

We decided to go to Boston, just in case. We called and asked the airport officials to wire the pilot of the Miami/Boston flight. At least, if she were on the plane, reassure her that we were coming.

We arrived at Logan around 1:00 am. Becky was standing outside the terminal, alone, except for two drunks on the bench behind her, tears streaming down her face. She had gotten the wrong message and had expected us to be there.

It is possible—with parents, grandparents, family, friends, the U.S. embassy and a large portion of the marines all searching for you and concerned about you—to feel terribly abandoned and alone.

Are you searching for me, God?

7/20/87

Depression

"Though I should walk through the valley of death, no evil will I fear."
—Psalm 23:4

. . . to Ellie, Vyki, and John

Underqualified for Commuting

It happened again today. The car veering wildly off the road jarred me awake at the steering wheel. It is no use pretending any more. I no longer have the energy to commute to the jobs for which I have spent my life preparing. I am educationally over-qualified for the area in which I live and physically underqualified for commuting.

10/1/87

Doctor of Ministry

I finished the degree. They all talked me into it. The doctor said I would someday regret the decision if I quit, because that would have been forced upon me by the illness. The seminary said I would be wasting four years of work, since there would be no culminating diploma to show for it. Ed said I would be throwing away the time and the money I had spent on my education. Even my boss encouraged me, believing the doctorate would add credibility to our office. And so I finished.

My resignation has been submitted. Illness has already stolen the one career for which my degree prepared me. I stand to receive my hood, exhausted and drained, feeling much like a mother who has spent herself to prepare a nursery for a child destined to be stillborn.

10/3/87

I'm Nobody

I am nobody. I thought I had lost my job, but I lost my identity. No one asks who I am, only what I do. Their eyes cloud over at my response, their faces barely masking their contempt, as they visibly dismiss any possibility of intelligence or creativity on my part. I do nothing. Therefore, I am nobody.

10/15/87

I'm Dead

Depression. More paralyzing by far than MS, it has fallen over me, enveloping me like a vacuum within a bell jar. People peer in, faces distorted as they press against the glass, but I can no longer hear what they are saying. They reach out to me but the wall of glass divides us. There are tears in their eyes, but I am beyond tears. I am numb.

What use is a life lived within a vacuum? What could the future possibly hold? Loved ones spending years polishing the glass in vain attempts to reach me. Weeks of uselessness stretching into months, and then years. Expensive life-support systems to sustain a life that was over long before. I'm dead. Can't you hear me? I'm dead! Would somebody please inform my body?

10/18/87

Pretending To Be Alive

We are editing the video we shot in September, a video to train leaders for my family program which has yet to be published. I watch, with a sense of wonder, the person on the tape. She looks so vibrant, so alive. No one would ever guess that I was dying. Why should they? They have yet to discover that I am dead.

Beside me, John works, unaware of the feelings that strangle me. High school drama director by profession and producer by desire, he has become my partner in this enterprise. He teases and laughs and prods us on, creating electronic miracles with dials and buttons. Occasionally, when the outcome surprises even us, he'll squeeze my hand. In that moment, I want desperately to hold on . . . to life, to his enthusiasm, to his belief that I might yet accomplish something worthwhile.

Don't let go, John! Can't you see I am slipping away? Can't you feel the wall of glass? Don't you know I am only pretending to be alive?

His eyes have turned back to the screen, his hands to the dials, as he asks for another tape. I respond and the game of make-believe continues. O God, give me the courage to stop pretending!

10/20/87

Ghosts

Today, I let Vyki know that I am dead. It was a mistake. The secret is more than she can bear. She was angry and afraid. Ghosts scare people who care.

11/2/87

Numb

Wallie came to visit me. I was at his church last week working on his computer, when he noticed. He knows I am dead, he just doesn't want to admit it. He swung at the bell jar wildly, shattering the glass and dragging me back. But the vacuum is inside me now. It is too late.

He wants me to visit his friend David, a member of his church, a psychologist. I am not sick in the head. I am dead. They just forgot to bury me. But I will go with him, so that he will let me rest in peace.

David, boy-wonder of Israel, I am afraid. I am no longer sure I want a hero to slay the giant that possesses me. Death has grown comfortable; the numbness is safe.

11/24/87

A Dangerous Man

David looks at me intently as he asks about my plan. Do I really intend to go through with it? Would I kill myself? What a strange question! How can you kill someone who is already dead? I only want them to bury me and get on with their lives.

This is a dangerous man. It would be too easy to talk to him, too easy, in his presence, to allow myself to feel again. Already, the hidden rage is welling up. I must get out of here.

11/25/87

If I scream . . .

David's room is small and square, with large windows. There are sounds of children in the background, but they are not my children. They do not know me. They will not be hurt if I scream. What a strange thought! Do I want to scream?

I thought that depressed people cried. But I don't want to cry. I want to smash things, to throw rocks through the windows, rip apart the couch, gouge holes in the hardwood floors. I want to pound on this quiet man with my fists until he bleeds.

Whatever made me think I was numb? I am consumed with rage. I am not dead; I am crazy.

11/28/87

A Middle Ground

David says that I'm not crazy; I'm not even sick. I have a right to be depressed. Anyone who has been slammed with a degenerative illness, watched her career slip away, realized the enormous emotional and financial burdens her life was suddenly putting on her family, *should* be depressed and absolutely furious. That's a healthy reaction. It's normal. I'm normal. (No one has ever accused me of that before!)

But there has to be a middle ground between venting the violent rage until it destroys all those I love and bottling it up until it destroys me. Perhaps, for now, David's room can be that middle ground, a place of sanctuary, where I am exempt from expectations and conventions, where it is safe to be enraged, where I can be set free.

You are not David at all. You are Daniel. Stay with me in the lion's den. If we can tame the beasts, perhaps I can survive.

12/1/87

Friendship

Why doesn't the depression leave? If I have faced the causes, expressed the anger, why am I not healed? The blackness still hovers around me. I am like a person who has had surgery for a malignancy, expecting to be cured, only to discover the long, painful road to recovery that lies ahead.

Another publisher rejected my family program. Ed tried to convince me that they were not rejecting *me*, and he gave me all the plausible reasons why this happened. But I suspect he is only saying these things because he loves me. I feel myself slipping back to the comforting protection of the numbness. John, as always the optimistic partner, was full of ideas. We will publish the program ourselves and market it with the video. We'll form a company and make lots of videos (and lots of money!). I am too numb, too tired to argue.

John took me to see a printer; I followed submissively. We are going to publish the program ourselves. John, you are a good friend. I know you are willing to expend your time, energy and income to help me find something to do that makes me feel worthwhile. But that's the problem, John. I have to stop basing my worth on what I do, because I face a future in which I may not be able to do anything at all. I need to believe that I am worthwhile simp-

ly because of who I am. In that, your friendship
will do more for me than all your plans will ever
accomplish.

12/5/87

The Spirit Within

For weeks, now, I have been startling myself awake at night. Each time I awake, I know I have been singing in my sleep, but the melody and words elude me.

Tonight, I clung tenaciously to the moment before waking and as I opened my eyes to the darkness, the song still hovered in the air.

> Thank you, God, for the gift of birth,
> For love made flesh to refresh the earth,
> For life and strength and length of days
> I give you thanks and praise.
>
> Your grace discovers me when my heart
> hides,
> Though I might run from you Your love
> abides.
>
> —S. Miriam Therese Winter

Maybe it is true that the Spirit within us prays when we no longer know how. I had given up on you, God. Why have you never given up on me?

12/10/87

Christmas, 1987

I didn't want to celebrate Advent this year. Ed put out the Advent wreath and faithfully lit the candles, but I could not pray. I have always seen myself as an Advent person, one of those who "wait in joyful hope." But there is no longer any joy in the future for which I wait. I have become a Lenten person, moving slowly but steadily toward crucifixion.

I am angered by the Christmas lights, by the anticipation in the children's faces. I feel cheated. Anticipation, for me, has become synonymous with dread.

Vyki gave me a calendar for Christmas, a quiet expression of hope that I would choose to survive another year.

12/25/87

Be a child . . .

Today we finally discovered what's been hurting Jon. One year of counselling had failed to unearth the secret that, in an unguarded moment, slipped out, unbidden and unexpected.

Ed and I were in the kitchen talking while Jon sat absorbed in his homework at the counter. Another absent-minded faux pas on Ed's part had set us laughing and he asked me jokingly, "Are you going to take care of me when I am old and senile?" I responded, "Who is going to take care of me? Jon, will you take care of me when I am old and senile?"

Caught completely off guard, he missed the laughter in our voices. He looked up, his eyes holding a misery I would not have thought possible in one so young. Tears quickly blurred his anguish as he said, "I can't, Mom. I'm sorry. I've thought it through a hundred times and I just can't. I can't handle it when you can't move. I would have to put you in a convalescent home. But I will take care of you financially, I promise."

My son, my son! What guilt have you lived with this last, incredible year? I would not leave the burden of such a decision on your shoulders at forty-six, let alone at sixteen. It has all been decided, the plans have all been made. Go free, exorcised of your guilt, and be a child again. Childhood will be over soon enough.

12/28/87

Love

God is love. A simple truth. All my growing up years I was taught this; now, suddenly, I discover I have never believed it. I said, "God is love," but what I meant was that God was loving. And when life proved unloving, I stopped believing.

If God is truly love, then God is the husband who fixes the meals and helps me in the shower, consistently believing in me, patiently (and not so patiently) putting up with me. God is the kids who still trust me, confide in me, and give me an important, though no longer central, place in their universe. God is the friend who had my house cleaned as a Christmas present, the partner who brought videos to make me laugh, the mother who took me to lunch, the family that supported me, the friends who challenged me out of my self-chosen death.

I have been looking for God in all the wrong places. God is not the storm that rages around me; God is the love that sustains me in its midst. God *is* love.

1/10/88

Letting Go

Pain is a carrier pigeon. Read the message it brings you, then set it free. Don't make a pet out of the bird.

... to the drama students at
Pomperaug High

Letting Go

I think that I am grieving. Everything moves me to tears. I am constantly seeking the comfort of Ed's arms around me. But why? It seems strange that I would stop believing I was dead, only to start grieving.

A part of me has died: some of my hopes and dreams, my plans for the future, my career. It is appropriate to grieve. Perhaps when I have finished grieving, I will be able to let go. Perhaps then I will make new plans, dream new dreams, and plant new hopes. Perhaps then I will cherish the memories, too painful yet for reflection.

1/12/88

Guilt

I wish someone had prepared me for the guilt. I had read Kulber-Ross and knew all about denial, anger, depression, and bargaining, even though I failed to recognize them in myself. But no one told me about the guilt.

I should have suspected it, back when Elizabeth's counselor told us Liz felt responsible for my illness. She had had a bad cold. I was guilty of saying nothing more than what every mother has said at some time to a coughing child. "Cover your mouth. Do you want someone else to get sick?" Well, someone else did get sick. Me. I not only got sick, I went into a hospital and came out in a wheelchair. Now no amount of reassurance or explanation can erase the guilt from her eyes.

I have watched each of my children blame themselves for my sickness, and I, in turn, have blamed myself for their guilt. I have begun to wonder if guilt is a way to control the uncontrollable. Convincing ourselves that we are responsible for what has happened allows us some sense of control, imaginary though it might be. Perhaps we need our guilt; it is less frightening than believing in a whimsical universe, or worse, a whimsical God.

It takes great maturity to let go of guilt, to accept the unacceptable because there is simply no alternative, and to get on with our lives. I think I need to grow up.

2/15/88

Anger

It takes an enormous amount of energy to be angry. I suspect, at one time, the anger was important, and fueled my drive for survival. But it has become destructive, sapping the strength that could be better spent on healing. It is time to let go of the anger. A quiet voice inside me keeps saying: "Make friends with your illness. You are going to walk a long, long way with it."

2/20/88

A Place of Refuge

Most would consider Pomperaug High a strange place of refuge. The massive brick structure on the hill has been accused of resembling a prison more than a school, an impression somewhat confirmed by the uniformed guard at the entrance. The masses of teenage humanity that periodically converge in its halls and cafeteria can be overwhelming to the uninitiated. It is a tinderbox of unconverted energy waiting to explode. It has also been my haven.

Teenagers are a brutally honest lot. While it is well within the code of teenage ethics to deceive someone in authority, they accept nothing less than the truth from their peers. I have discovered I am free to be myself among them. Constant cheerfulness and unlimited patience are not expected of me here. Discouragement, anger, peevishness, silliness, joy, are all acceptable. Dishonesty is the only thing that is not.

I came to the drama department to help out a little, to give John some of the time he has given me. I have become a permanent fixture. The kids have affectionately dubbed me Drama Mom. It is a good name. Like "Moms" everywhere, I run the errands, drive the carpools, avert last minute catastrophes, and do the little things everyone else has forgotten, things that frequently remain unthanked and unnoticed. I get to offer comfort, support and a little counsel to kids who twirl my canes, race my scooter, discuss my disability, and love me for who I am.

I suspect I may be doing something worthwhile. I think my presence at the school may be important to these kids. I know it has been important to me.

3/1/88

"Support" Staff

The maintenance people at the school are terrific. They share bits of family news, tease me about my canes, and play policeman to my scooter. Their presence brings a strange sense of comfort and reassurance.

3/6/88

Who Changed?

One of the people in the main office asked me about the MS, specifically about the fluctuations in my mobility. The room grew uncomfortably quiet and I could feel the tension in the silence. I started to explain softly why on some days I looked fine while on others I was quite disabled. It was such a relief to talk openly about something everyone had politely tried to ignore, that the words were soon tumbling over each other. Several people chimed in at once with questions I had read so often in their eyes, but which they had never dared to ask. I was soon recounting some of my more ignominious mishaps and we were laughing together.

Tonight I am wondering what enabled Terri to ask that question. Have they changed? Has their attitude toward my disability changed? Or have I changed? Have I become comfortable enough with myself that others can now risk being comfortable with me? Perhaps a little of both.

3/11/88

Flashback

Just when I thought I could see the light at the end of the tunnel, the darkness has enveloped me again. It is like a flashback, depression just as severe, just as overwhelming. But this time I cried out for help.

My Mom was there for me. She did not give advice or analyze or direct. She and my Dad offered me the money for a trip to Bermuda. How many times have I cried out in the night and you have answered me? How many times have you surprised me with your unexpected, unpredictable, wonderful responses? Can I ever be for my children the unselfish, loving people you have been in my life?

Vyki and I are going to Bermuda. She is only on vacation until the end of March, so we have to move quickly. The travel agents thought we were crazy, but Vyki was undaunted and called the airlines and hotels herself. We leave next week.

3/13/88

Bermuda

Bermuda was wonderful. Our hotel room had a small balcony overlooking a beautiful blue-green bay. It was there that I enjoyed the sunrise, while Vyki captured the opportunity to sleep late. We rented mopeds one day, strapped my cane to the basket, and tentatively tried the hotel driveway to see if I was going to have difficulty balancing. I did fine; it was Vyki who ran up the embankment and wiped out in the bushes!

At nearby Horseshoe Bay, we explored the rocks and coastline, then lay huddled up on the beach. (Bermuda is not that warm in March!) We walked down to the ocean at night to watch the waves crashing against the rocks, the whitened foam catching a sprinkle of light from the hotel above. It was only three days, but time enough for talking and sharing, and time enough for solitude and silence.

It was in the silence that I began to realize just how much Ed has suffered through my illness and depression. I knew it before; I simply could not bear to deal with it. Solitude and space remind me of my love.

We spend all of our lives working at becoming in control. From the first time we cry as infants and someone responds, we are learning to control our environment. Our first smiles, first attempts to crawl, first words, first steps, and toilet training—all are a process of coming to control. I am gradually being deprived of what I have spent a lifetime learning. I have been coping with a disease that contains the potential of returning me to infancy.

What I have not allowed myself to realize is that my parents chose to have an infant; my husband did not. Is it any wonder that 78% of the marriages of those diagnosed with MS end in divorce? Ed, too, has been losing control. I have leaned so heavily on him for support, I have forgotten to give mine.

Thank you, Mom and Dad. Once again, you have given me life.

Thank you, Vyki, for sustaining that life with your friendship.

Thank you, Ed, for filling that life with your love.

3/27/88

Speechless

The Rabbit broke down out of state. While the garage worked at getting it running, Ed and I decided to eat at a small restaurant across the street. The meal was passable; the service okay. The problem came when I needed to use the restroom.

It was an old building, and the waiter pointed up a steep, ladder-like staircase. No, there was no elevator. I struggled up the stairs, half-sitting, half-crawling, only to find a beautiful, wheelchair accessible lavatory. Except that no wheelchair could have ever reached it!

On later questioning, I was told the law required a wheelchair accessible stall within every restroom. It did not require that the room itself be wheelchair accessible. I'm speechless.

4/4/88

Too Late

Today I heard from a publisher who wants my program. Where were you six months ago when I so desperately needed you? I needed someone to tell me that what I had done was worthwhile, that it was acceptable to my church, that I was acceptable. When my future was ripped away, I needed to know that my past had not been wasted. Where were you then?

You can have the program. You can have it because I am tired of trips to the post office, handling orders, making copies, advertising, and answering calls. You can have it because I am tired of all the work the program involves, not because I need you to affirm its acceptability or my own worth as a person. You are too late for that.

4/21/88

Remembering Me

Ed has become a drama widower. As the play approaches, I become more and more absorbed at the school. I had forgotten how much I loved the theater. I have forgotten too many things about myself. Strange, in a world of make-believe I should discover so much of the real me.

5/1/88

Again, and yet again . . .

Once again, the depression comes. I know it was brought on by our trip south to look for colleges for Jon. I am terrified that we will not have the money, that my illness has deprived my very bright children of the chance of a great education. Ed, the realist, says you apply anywhere you want to go and wait and see who offers you money. He keeps pointing out it is too early to get depressed!

But my depression is not reasonably chosen. It comes in waves, overpowering me unexpectedly. This time, however, I am not as frightened. This time I know it will pass. I will remember the lesson of Bermuda. I will hold on to those who love me. I will be good to myself and wait.

5/16/88

Drama Banquet

There was a banquet for the drama students. These kids have become an important part of my life. I may have come to drama because of my friendship with John; I have stayed because of my love for them.

6/26/88

"Sicked Upon"

I have discovered that March 1, 1986, has become the point around which I date everything else. I continually refer to things as happening before or after I "got sick." Ellie told me today that it was a horrible choice of words.

" 'Got sick' sounds as if you went out looking for it. You didn't get sick. You got 'sicked upon'!"

"Before I got sicked upon . . ."—I like it!

It is strange, Ellie, that I find you so seldom in this journal. The pages of my life are filled with you. Perhaps the best friends are those whose presence is so faithful it is almost unnoticed . . . but never unappreciated.

7/1/88

Telephone Books

I did it again! I took on a job far too demanding, far too exhausting for my limited physical strength. I want so much to be a contributing member of my family, a financially contributing member. However, delivering phone books is not going to be it!

Liz had come with me, hoping to earn a little money. By the time we had negotiated several stairways, arms heaped with the heavy books, even she was exhausted. I was crippled. We managed to cap the day off by locking the keys in the car and having to wait for two hours to be rescued.

The company responsible for delivering the books did not want to take them back. Only when it became clear that no amount of coercion was going to make me physically able to accomplish this task, did they condescend to retrieve them.

Tonight, I am dependent on my scooter to get so far as the bathroom. Why do I continue to make such unrealistic demands on myself?

7/2/88

Volleyball

We spent the Fourth with the Sabo's, the day culminating in a rousing family game of volleyball. As I sat on the sidelines and watched, I was struck by the fact that all of these people whom I know and love so well, played volleyball much the same way that they lived.

My Jon, John and Beau Sabo were on one team; Ed, Vyki, Liz and Becky were on the other. Beau practically played by himself, entering the game with a vengeance, diving for balls not in his territory, knocking down his own teammates in his effort to get to the ball first. It didn't take long before he started feeling tired and a little resentful toward his teammates. Sorry, Beau, but sometimes we don't allow others to help us.

Jon, on the other hand, stood patiently waiting for the ball to come to him, hitting fairly accurately the few times Beau didn't get there first. It isn't enough to be good, Jon. Sometimes in life we have to take risks and make our opportunities.

Elizabeth kept being distracted by whether or not she was on the right side. Relationships will always be more important to her than the game.

Becky kept needing to explain why she had missed a shot. In her world, things are acceptable as long as they are reasonable. No one was really listening.

The adults were a little more subtle in their play, but still fairly obvious. Ed and Vyki were both concerned about the rules, but for different reasons. If Vyki was going to play, she was going to play fair. If Ed was going to play, he was going to win. John simply didn't care. He just wanted to play and in his effort to keep the game moving, he had a tendency to run roughshod on the rulemakers. All perfectly in keeping with how these three adults live their lives.

And what of me? Is it my role to sit on the sidelines and watch others play, becoming critical because I cannot take part? Perhaps my role is to reflect on the experience and capture it in words for those too busy participating to have time for reflecting.

7/4/88

Camp Winnie

Camp Winnie. Whatever possessed me to say I would give a course in this God-forsaken family campground? They said it was "handicapped accessible." I guess if your handicap is hearing, you might manage here! Why is it so hard for people who can walk to realize how far away things are for people who can't? "All on one level" it may be, but the walks on the level are riddled with protruding roots and rocks to trip a cane or dragging foot. "Ramp to the dining room" if you can call a 70-degree incline a ramp. For me, it is more inaccessible than a stairway. Able-bodied people can be so insensitive.

Why do I do this? Why can't I simply accept the fact that I am crippled and stop venturing out into unknown space, expecting, by some miracle, to overcome my limits?

8/6/88

Limited

Today, I am ashamed. People are not insensitive to my needs, only ignorant of them. And if I am too proud to share them, whose fault is that? I do not want to believe that I am limited; I hate being confronted with my limits. But the only other choice is to hide away in the safe world of the known, and probably die of boredom.

It is possible to function in a foreign world of able-bodied people, if I give them the opportunity to help me, if I am humble enough to admit to needing their help. It isn't a crime to complain; it isn't a crime to be needy. The only crime is to allow the need to become an excuse for not living.

Multiple sclerosis has crippled my body. I had no choice in that. I *can* choose whether or not I will allow fear and pride to cripple my spirit.

8/7/88

Manipulation

I have discovered something important here at Camp Winnie. It is not just that I am ashamed of letting people know my limits, I am terrified of using those limits to manipulate others. But I think I have also discovered the difference.

I can say:

"The ramp to the dining room is just too steep for me. I know I can't manage it."

Your possible suggestions:

"I'll let you know when I am going to meals and help you."

"Someone can bring you a tray."

"Maybe we could get a wheelchair."

"Why don't you just drive into town and buy your meals, if it's such a problem."

My typical response:

"I can manage the ramp. Don't worry about me. Oops! Thanks for catching me. No, you don't have to be here. I'll be fine, just take my hand this time."

Now, your only possible response to this is to be aware whenever I am making the dangerous journey down the ramp. You are not free to suggest something that would work better for you, or to schedule a time agreeable for both of us, because I have already pointed out that I don't need you. Of

93

course, you could allow me to get hurt, but usually when we do this, we know the other will be trapped by guilt into being available. That's manipulation!

I suspect manipulation is cornering others in such a way that their only possible response is the one we have already chosen. Disabled people may not have a monopoly on the manipulation market, but we certainly have a distinct advantage. Those around us already feel guilty simply by reason of the fact that they are well and we are not. It is a great temptation to use that guilt for our own ends.

Owning our limits actually leaves others free. Simply and honestly stating our needs gives others the opportunity to respond, or not respond, in any manner they choose. I may not always like their response, but far more importantly, I will like myself.

8/8/88

The Health Spa

Today I visited Holiday Matrix. The doctor felt that swimming would help my legs, and the nearest lap pool was at the fitness spa. It was like entering a temple to the human body. The air was heavy with the incense of human sweat, and the organ swell that greeted my ears was the thump-thumping of weights, machinery and feet. I was the only one who had arrived at the feast without a wedding garment. Everyone else was properly attired in Nike tights and leotards, running shorts and gel-air shoes. All seemed to have chosen outfits that showed off their muscled curvature to the greatest advantage. It was difficult to understand why any of these beautiful people needed to work out at all. They averted their eyes quickly as I entered with my cane, as if visual contact with me could somehow lead to contamination. It was going to be hard to find a god of mercy who would lower me into the pool to be healed. I left quickly, feeling naked and ashamed.

It was not that I had not met these communicants before. The ones who worship privately, I see daily on the roads, less formal in their attire, but still a constant reminder of my infirmity. It was finding them in such large numbers, concentrated in one small place, that overwhelmed me. It would be difficult in the face of gods such as these to feel whole if you were twenty pounds overweight!

I have decided against swimming at Holiday Matrix. Whatever it might do for my legs, it would not be worth the damage it would inflict upon my spirit.

12/4/88

Next Time

I went Christmas shopping without my scooter. A fatal mistake! The catastrophe happened in Sears. Someone brushed by me, dislodging my cane, and the exhausted balance button within my brain refused to function. I fell into a rack of bathrobes, bringing everything down in a chaotic pile on top of me. I peered up through the robes to find more than a dozen concerned faces staring down at me.

Describing the incident later to Jean, she said: "Next time, Kathy, pull out a robe from the bottom, hold it up and yell, 'I found it!' "

Next time!

12/13/88

Gifts

I remember taking my children to be vaccinated. They screamed their resentment lustily, that I should allow someone to hurt them in such a manner. My own childhood had been plagued with the diseases against which I was now offering them protection. But their little minds were far too small to understand or to appreciate the gift. I held them in my arms, and cried with them in their pain.

Is it too much to believe in a God who offers gifts far beyond my comprehension, then cradles me lovingly and weeps for my pain?

1/18/89

The Perfect Response

What can people say when I tell them I have a degenerative illness? They can't tell me they hope I feel better; most of the time I am feeling as well as I am going to get. But I wish I could find a better response than the ones I usually receive. I am tired of the pity:

"I'm so sorry!"

the incredulity:

"But you look perfectly fine!"

the piousness:

"God's will is so strange."

worst of all, the canonization:

"God knows the ones who can bear it," and "You're such a special person."

But what's the alternative?

I was substituting at the high school, zipping around on my little scooter, when I ran into (literally!) one of the school's perennial "problems."

"Hey, Missus Chesto! You oughta be careful. How come you ride that thing around anyway? Somethin's wrong with your legs?"

"I have multiple sclerosis."

"Oh yeah? What's that?"

I explained, simply, that it is a disease that causes the nervous system to fail, eventually interfering with walking and other functions. The burly figure towered over me, his face softening with a strange mixture of compassion and pain.

He spoke softly, "Man, is that shitty!"

The perfect response!

2/28/89

The "Benefits"

There was a core of people visiting the high school today from IBM. Mike, the assistant principal, was showing them around when we met at the elevator. They looked down at the scooter and at me with that mixture of curiosity and pity that makes normal conversation almost impossible. But Mike was equal to the moment.

"This is Kathy Chesto, one of our substitutes. What do you think of her mode of transportation? We may not pay our substitutes much, but the benefits are terrific!"

Thanks, Mike, I owe you one.

4/7/89

Running Is Like That

Jon is cleaning his room in preparation for college. I was helping him sort through memorabilia when I got caught up in reading his own account of his life in his heritage paper. Here is a teenager whose shelves are lined with the trophies he has won racing, yet, with his usual realism and humor, the race he described as most important to him was one he lost.

"Perhaps one of the best moments in all of my track career was freshman year at the Western Connecticut Conference Championships . . . I was told to run the two mile because we had only one other runner in it. After a few laps, I was obviously the candidate for last place, with the rest of the pack a good distance in front of me. After a while, a lot of the girls felt sorry for me and started cheering me on. Soon, the crowd of 800 spectators started to get into it (maybe because it was the last race and they were anxious for me to finish so they could leave.) It was a euphoric feeling, as I pulled into the last 100 meter stretch under the glow of the lights with the huge crowd cheering for me. Many of the spectators delivered a standing ovation as I raced by. The time I got when I crossed the finish line was my personal best and our freshman record, despite the fact that I finished dead last. Running is like that."

Not only running, Son, but life. I need your humor, your wonderful sense of self. I hope I can remember that personal best is personal best, even when it's dead last.

8/3/89

Resenting Life

I don't think I ever really liked my job. I loved the people in the diocesan office; Gerry was wonderful to me in so many ways. I loved the opportunities to meet people, the credibility that went with the title, the sense of identity and the paycheck. But I don't think I ever really liked being an administrator.

I like writing. I like travelling and giving talks. I like the freedom to be my own person, to speak my own truth, to represent no one. Why did I cling so tenaciously to a job that had so little power to satisfy me? It was not that I wanted it, only that I resented its being taken away.

8/16/89

Surfing Belly-down

Vacation. Such a wonderful invention! We played in the surf yesterday, allowing the waves to buffet us and wash us into shore. A few people stopped to stare at my canes. That's okay, folks. You should see me when I do this with a walker!

Today, the sea is wild after the storm. Choppy waves crash against eroding sands, turning the coastline white with foam. The sunbathers and beachcombers have all been driven away; only those who take the sea seriously are on its shores today.

The surfers are out in force. My heart is drawn to them, although I know my body well enough to realize it could not withstand the ocean's rage. There are those who skim effortlessly along the surface of the violent waves, but my kinship is with those who tumble, again and again, into the turbulent water. I laugh in recognition when they choose to ride belly-down on their boards, undaunted by their limits, conquering the sea any way they can. After all, it isn't the form that counts, but the joy of the ride.

8/18/89

Common Grief

Jon has left for college. Even if we did not know that fact only too well, the signs all around would inform us. There are no more running shoes in the entry way, with the scent of the sportsman hovering over them. The house is strangely silent with the absence of teenage boys. The walls and floors no longer vibrate with the sounds of "Yes" and "Genesis," and the telephone rings a little less frequently, despite the two girls left behind him. There is hot water in the shower, dry towels in the bathroom, gas in the car, cookies in the cookie jar, and juice in the fridge. The meat spoils and the bread goes moldy when we forget we are adjusting not to one less mouth but to five thousand less calories a day.

It is possible, once again, to walk into his room. The mural he painted so assiduously is the strongest remaining trace of the boy turned man. Blank spots on the wall, vacated by beloved posters gone to college, stare down at me, like vacant eyes. The closet is empty of clothes; the display of high school trophies and plaques looks lonely on the shelf behind the pole. Gone is the clutter of books and papers, records and tapes, clean laundry and dirty socks. The only thing left on the floor is dust.

Jon has gone to Wesleyan. Our son has gone away. Are we sad? Yes, oh yes!

There is a normalcy about this grief that is comforting. This time, we do not face the pain alone. Every parent who has ever said good-bye to a child has probably done so with the same mixture of reluctance and relief. This time, our grief is common, but that does not make it any less painful.

9/3/89

Treasure the Now

I have begun to think differently about time, how uncertain it is, how precious, how fragile. Each of us is dying of a terminal illness; it's called "life." I am one of the fortunate ones, forced to confront the fragility. As the pain gradually eases, I discover a beauty in the moment possible only because it is so fleeting. The great lesson of degenerative illness is the lesson life itself tries to teach all of us: TREASURE THE NOW.

9/5/89

Life-Maps

Life's journeys would be so much easier if we came supplied with a map! Please don't give me that pious prattle about the Bible being the Great Map. The Bible has given me all kinds of insight into God. It is insight into *me* that seems to be lacking.

I find myself returning over and over again to the same spot, not because it is the right path, but because I have gotten lost and walked around in a circle again. Still, perhaps I bring a little more knowledge to this moment. At least, this time, I recognize that I am lost.

9/20/89

Epilogue

This is a book without a conclusion, without an ending, a book about a process, the process of hoping. It has only just begun. Am I healed? Yes. Do I still have multiple sclerosis? Yes.

The diagnosis of MS has become a pivotal point in my life; so much has come to hinge on the time I "got sicked upon." Degenerative illness has forced upon me risks I would never have had the courage to take, had I believed in a secure tomorrow. The crippling of my body has allowed me to let go of much that was crippling my spirit. When I was no longer able to define myself in terms of what I did, I became freer to discover who I am.

Unfortunately, freedom is often terrifying. Several years back, a wonderful cartoon depicted Garfield staring mournfully through a pet store window at all the animals in their cages. Suddenly, he announced: "This is a job for Super Cat," and ran through the store opening all the cages, shouting: "You're free! You're free!" But the animals all cowered in the corners. Garfield reflected briefly, then returned, slamming the doors shut and shouting: "You're secure! You're secure!" The price of freedom is security. I would never have chosen to pay it, but life left me no choice.

Freedom would have been unbearable without love. The family who supported me, the close friends who were able to bear the pain, and the students at the high school who knew nothing at all about me but loved me anyway—all played a far greater role in my healing than this limited book could ever express.

I can no longer work in an office and bring home a regular paycheck, but I can write, make videos, substitute teach, travel, and give talks. I may not be extraordinarily successful in any one of these areas, but I have learned to live fully today. I have no way of knowing if I will have a tomorrow.

MS is very much with me. I struggle with periodic depression, but I have learned that it will pass. I am embarrassed by loss of bladder control, terrified by loss of memory, and frustrated by loss of mobility, but there is no one else I would rather be.

Would I like to be cured? Oh yes, but not at the cost of all I have learned. I have come face to face with the unfathomable, unchangeable God, and I have found that while I may not always like it, I can live with the mystery.

If I had those years to live over, would I do it differently? You bet I would!

I would cry more on the outside
And hurt less on the inside
Next time.

I would yell more at the doctors
And less at my family
Next time.

I would protect others less
And trust them more
Next time.

I would be more courageous at taking
   risks
But more honest about my limits
Next time.

I would work less at being good
And harder at being healthy
Next time.

And I would never forget
There is always a Next Time.
It's called TODAY.

Afterword:
Distinguished Alumna?

The computer monitor stared at me, the control icons stretching across the top of the page, mocking the emptiness of the screen. In three hours, the seminary that had granted me a doctorate would be giving me their distinguished alumnae award and I still had no idea what I would say. I simply did not feel very distinguished.

The alumni chairman had first called our home while I was on retreat and I had quickly second-guessed the meaning of his message. When my traveling had forced me to resign from the council, I had offered to do one-time tasks that could be completed in my own time frame. Two years had passed and someone was finally taking me up on the offer. I was happy to be asked and delighted when the chairman called back.

After the initial introductions, we had entered into an animated discussion about mutual friends and professors. I should have realized he knew a lot more about me than I would have had reason to expect. He had asked about the MS and I answered simply that I was doing well. There are no words to explain the wonder I feel every time I get out of bed in the morning and my legs hold me up, my eyes focus, and I can even remember what I ate for supper the night before. Years ago, I stopped burdening people with an excitement they couldn't possibly understand.

The conversation drifted to the award. So this was it. They wanted me to find a plaque and take care of getting it engraved. The chairman went on about the importance of the award, how carefully the recipient was chosen, the honor it bestowed – the way we always stress the importance of a task when we are enlisting volunteers. I wanted to interrupt and tell him he didn't need to do that, I had decided I would help before he had called and I already had three phone books on the counter with the yellow pages open to "awards." I was halfway down the column in the Danbury book and only partly listening when he said, "We have chosen you as this year's distinguished alumna." Caught completely offguard, I said the only thing I could think to say: "Why?"

My question was greeted with a moment of stunned silence, a few sputtered sentences of explanation, and finally the incredulous remark, "I wasn't expecting you to ask that. People don't usually say that!" Of course they don't. With one word, I had managed to discredit the award, the council and my own life!

I had recovered from the moment as graciously as possible under the circumstances, but now, with the blank computer screen in front of me, I was still asking the same question. Why?

I wandered out to the living room. Becky had stayed home from her social services job at HeadStart, trying to recover enough from the flu to be able to attend the evening ceremony. She was curled up in blankets sipping chicken soup. Liz was on the couch buried in chemistry notes and books, preparing for a midterm. She had taken the day off from her pre-med classes at NYU to celebrate with us, but the exam was tomorrow and time was short.

I presented my dilemma. "I don't feel very distinguished. I never really set out to do any of the things that happened. Everything sort of happened to me. What do I say?"

Becky glanced up from her soup, looking far too sick and too miserable for the question to matter very much at the moment.

"How about 'Thank-you'?"

"It has a nice ring to it, Becky, but the speech is scheduled to last ten minutes. I think you are supposed to include all that stuff about what got you to this point. That's my problem. What did get me to this point?"

Liz pulled her attention away from the chemistry.

"Mom," she said, "just tell them your life is a metathesis reaction."

"What?" That helped a lot. "Maybe you had better stick to the chemistry."

"No, seriously, Mom. A metathesis reaction has two forms, endothermic and exothermic. An endothermic reaction is one in which a substance draws energy from the other substances that touch it, and the substance itself changes as a result, creating heat in the process. Your life is like that. Everything that has come into it – your family, your illness, your car accident, all the things that have happened to us kids – you couldn't change any of it. But you managed to draw energy from it, and you allowed it to change you. That's endothermic.

"In an exothermic reaction the substance itself does not change, but it changes the substances that it touches, and that reaction gives off heat. Your life has been like that too. You have reached out to other people and even though you could never become part of their lives, they have been changed just because you touched them. So your life is also an exothermic reaction. Normally, in a metathesis reaction, they don't both happen at the same time, but in your life, I think they do. So, just tell them your life is an endothermic/exothermic reaction."

I wandered back to the computer. It was a good metaphor but I wanted to believe that my life hadn't been as much reaction as it had been response. Perhaps I was a catalyst. But a catalyst remains unchanged by the reaction it precipitates, and I have been changed by everything that has touched me and everything I have reached out to touch. Endothermic and exothermic. . . .

The telephone rang, bringing me back with a start. It was my son, offering congratulations, telling me how sorry he was that he could not be with us. The graduate school of journalism at Columbia was cramming a week of work into every Monday and he could not afford to miss that day. His love would be there.

I hung up, shaking off the shiver of fear his voice still evokes over the phone. It had been more than a year since the elderly gentleman, disoriented with Alzheimer's, had stepped in front of my son's car and been killed. But the nightmares persisted. The image of my son, staring at the world through frightened, haunted eyes as the flashbacks waged war with his sanity, always came crashing back with the sound of his voice and a simple "Hi, Mom." The memory of those terrible days of waiting and fear, when we discovered the legal system seemed to care more for vengeance than for justice, still lurked at the tip of my subconscious, ready to explode into rage with the slightest provocation. There had been two accidents in our family that year, both involving elderly men with Alzheimer's. But the crash that had left me with another permanent disability had done far less damage to our family than this accident that had robbed us of our peace.

There was a time when I thought I knew what hope meant. I thought I understood the risk. But too many nights of praying to a heaven that seemed empty from a heart even more hollow, too many days of wondering if my son would survive the pain, had left me questioning if I believed in anything at all, myself, my family, least of all, God. The words from Romans that had never before made sense, "These sufferings bring patience, patience brings perseverance, and perseverance brings hope," (5:4) slowly took on meaning. I had thought of hope as more active somehow. But in that awful darkness, when there was nothing left to do but hold on to one another tightly, hope found us.

People all across the United States and Canada, people who had formed my workshops, read my books, and celebrated my retreats, surrounded us in a circle of caring and support. Loving words of encouragement were sent to my son from people he had never met and would never know. Like an elusive butterfly, the hope that had escaped us as we thrashed about in anger came to rest gently on us, this time a hope born of patient endurance.

I was not feeling very distinguished, only very honored to have been loved so much. There is a legend from intertestamental times that states that at any given moment there are thirty "just ones" living on the earth, thirty people whose sheer goodness and prayer prevent the world from self-destructing. Like the ten "just ones" who could have saved the cities of Sodom and Gomorrah, their purity and love keep the wrath of God at bay and save the rest of us. If my life had been distinguished by anything at all, it was by the number of the "just ones" I had been privileged to know.

The speech was still unwritten when Ed arrived home and it was time for us to leave, but I finally knew what it was I wanted to say. Becky was right after all, but it had taken both Liz and Jon to remind me of the truth. All I really needed to say was "Thank-you" to all those distinguished people who had filled and shaped my life. Science calls it metathesis; faith calls it resurrection.

When Ed and I got married, a friend had made us a banner that we hung, first in the sanctuary for our wedding and later in the entrance of our home. The banner eventually succumbed to the ravages of time, but years of reading the message every time we came through our door has left the words engraved deeply in out hearts:

> For all that has been, "Thanks."
> To all that will be, "Yes."

10/16/95